DEMCO

THE LIBRARY OF
WOLVES AND WILD DOGS

THE ETHIOPIAN WOLF

Fred H. Harrington

The Rosen Publishing Group's
PowerKids Press™
New York

1-03

To David Macdonald. If Ethiopian wolves continue to survive in the wild,
it will be largely due to the hard work and dedication of scientists like him.

Published in 2002 by The Rosen Publishing Group, Inc.
29 East 21st Street, New York, NY 10010

First Edition

Book Design: Michael de Guzman
Project Editor: Emily Raabe

Photo Credits: pp. 4, 8, 12, 14, 16, 19, 20, © Claudio Sillero Zubari; p. 7 © Nicole Duplaix/Peter Arnold Inc.;
p. 11 © Raymond A. Mendez/Animals Animals.

Harrington, Fred H.
  The Ethiopian wolf /author, Fred H. Harrington.
    p. cm. — (The library of wolves and wild dogs)
  ISBN 0–8239–5767–5 (library binding)
1. Canis simensis—Juvenile literature. [1. Ethiopian wolf. 2. Wolves.] I. Title. II. Series.
  QL737.C22 H3665 2002
  599.77'2–dc21
                                                                    00–012983

Manufactured in the United States of America

Contents

1 What Are Ethiopian Wolves? 5

2 Why a Wolf Was Called a Jackal 6

3 How We Know They Are Wolves 9

4 A Different Kind of Prey 10

5 A Smaller Territory 13

6 Doing Things as a Group 14

7 Family Life 17

8 A Different Kind of Family 18

9 Ethiopian Wolves Are Endangered 21

10 Plans to Save the Wolves 22

Glossary 23

Index 24

Web Sites 24

What Are Ethiopian Wolves?

In the whole world today, there are only three kinds of wolves. These three types are gray wolves, red wolves, and Ethiopian wolves. Gray wolves are found all around the Northern Hemisphere. That means they live in North America, Greenland, Europe, Asia, and India. Red wolves also live in North America. Gray wolves and red wolves are similar in many ways. They are big animals, although gray wolves are a bit bigger than red wolves. They both live in packs and hunt large animals, such as deer, for food. Ethiopian wolves are different from gray or red wolves. Ethiopian wolves are much smaller than the other two kinds of wolves. They live in packs like other wolves, but they hunt by themselves. They are also the only wolves that live in Africa.

 Ethiopian wolves live high up in the mountains in the country of Ethiopia. They are extremely rare.

Why a Wolf Was Called a Jackal

Other kinds of wild dogs also live in Africa, such as African hunting dogs and jackals. Until recently, scientists thought Ethiopian wolves were a type of jackal. They gave Ethiopian wolves names like Semien jackal, Simenian jackal, or Ethiopian jackal. There are several reasons why scientists believed that Ethiopian wolves were jackals. First, Ethiopian wolves are much smaller than gray wolves. Second, gray wolves are stocky, with wide heads and muzzles, but Ethiopian wolves have long legs, long muzzles, and slender noses, as do jackals. Third, Ethiopian wolves eat mostly **rodents**, which jackals also love to eat. Fourth, Africa is where all three other kinds of jackals live. These are the reasons why it made sense to call a small, slender, wild dog from Africa a jackal.

Jackals, like the one shown here, are a little smaller than Ethiopian wolves. Local people still call Ethiopian wolves "ky kebero," which means "red jackal."

How We Know They Are Wolves

Today we know that Ethiopian wolves are really wolves, not jackals. In the 1990s, scientists began to study Ethiopian wolves' **genes**. When animals have similar genes, scientists believe they are closely related. Ethiopian wolves have genes that are similar to those of gray wolves and coyotes. Their genes are not similar to jackals' genes, however. Scientists now believe that thousands of years ago, gray wolves came to Africa from Europe or Asia. These wolves lived in mountains covered with grasses and shrubs. These plants provided food for small rodents. The wolves ate these small rodents. As the wolves **adapted** to their new **environment**, they became smaller and redder. They began to look like the jackals that lived in similar **habitats** and ate similar **prey**.

Even though the Ethiopian wolf (left) might look like a jackal, its closest relatives are gray wolves and coyotes.

A Different Kind of Prey

One of the biggest differences between Ethiopian wolves and gray wolves is their diet. Gray wolves like to hunt animals that are larger than they are, such as deer or moose. Ethiopian wolves hunt animals that are smaller than they are. Their favorite prey are grass rats and molerats. Grass rats are very common rodents where Ethiopian wolves live. Sometimes the wolves hunt in the middle of herds of cattle, so the rats don't see them coming. Ethiopian wolves also catch other types of rodents, hares, and birds. Because Ethiopian wolves hunt little animals, the wolves don't need to be very big. They also don't need to hunt in a pack like gray wolves. Sometimes Ethiopian wolves hunt in groups when they chase young antelopes or lambs, but usually Ethiopian wolves hunt alone.

Molerats live underground, where they eat roots. Ethiopian wolves hunt them during the day by digging them out of the ground.

A Smaller Territory

Every wolf pack lives in its own area, called a **territory**. In North America, gray wolf packs have territories that can be from 25 square miles (65 sq km) to larger than 400 square miles (1,036 sq km). Gray wolves need large territories so they can find enough prey to catch and eat. Ethiopian wolf packs have very small territories. Their territories are only 2 to 5 square miles (5 to 13 sq km) in size. They don't need a big territory, because their prey are small and there are lots of them. There are so many rodents that sometimes the wolves catch more than they can eat. When this happens, they hide the extra ones by burying them in the ground, just like squirrels bury acorns. This is called caching. When the wolves get hungry later, they know right where to find their caches of food!

 This Ethiopian wolf is digging stored food out of its cache.

Doing Things as a Group

Even though Ethiopian wolves don't hunt their prey in groups like other wolves, they still live in a pack and do things together as a group. Ethiopian wolves live in packs with 3 to 13 adults and 1 to 6 puppies. At night, the whole pack rests together. After they wake up in the morning, they **patrol** their territory as a group. All the older wolves help mark their territory

with scent to keep other packs away, just like gray wolves do. When they spot smaller packs, they chase them away. When the wolves finish patrolling their territory, they separate to hunt. They may come together again at midday to rest, and then separate to hunt alone in the afternoon. Each time they get together, Ethiopian wolves greet each other excitedly, noisily chasing about and licking each other's **muzzles**. They also spend time playing when they are together in a group.

These Ethiopian wolves are patrolling their territory.

Family Life

Ethiopian wolf packs are family groups. Packs start when a male and female meet, find a territory, **mate**, and have puppies. The puppies are born in a den dug in the ground, under a large rock, or in a rocky crevice. During their first month, they only drink milk. As they get older, their packmates feed them more and more **regurgitated** food. This means that older wolves bring back food in their stomachs. When they return, the pups greet them by licking the adult's muzzle. This causes the adults to regurgitate, or throw up, the food in their stomachs. It sounds gross, but it probably tastes great to a hungry baby wolf! When the puppies are one year old, they help to raise the next litter of puppies. They guard the den, chase away intruders, and feed and **groom** the new puppies.

These Ethiopian wolf pups are begging for food by licking the adult wolf's muzzle.

17

A Different Kind of Family

When gray wolves are about two or three years old, the young wolves usually leave the pack and try to start their own pack by finding a mate. This is true for both males and females. With Ethiopian wolves, however, only young females ever leave the pack. Young males stay with the pack for the rest of their lives! This creates a big problem for a young male. Where can he find a mate? He solves this problem by looking for a female that lives in another pack. When he finds a female, they mate but they don't stay together. Instead, he returns to his own pack and helps his mother raise her next **litter** of puppies. His mate returns to her own pack, where her sons or brothers help to raise her puppies.

These Ethiopian wolf puppies will stay together with their pack for at least two years before they head out on their own. If they are male puppies, they will probably stay with their childhood pack for the rest of their lives.

Ethiopian Wolves Are Endangered

Scientists first discovered Ethiopian wolves in the mountains of Ethiopia in 1835. These wolves were uncommon even then. The wolves lived high in mountain valleys and plateaus above 10,000 feet (3,048 m). When native Ethiopian people moved into these high mountain valleys, they often used the land where the wolves lived. These new settlers also brought their domestic dogs with them. Some of these dogs ran free and mated with wolves, so fewer purebred wolves were left. The settlers' dogs carried diseases, such as rabies and distemper, that can kill the wolves. Wolves also were killed by cars or by people with guns. Today only about 400 Ethiopian wolves are left in Ethiopia. These rare and beautiful wolves are in great danger of becoming **extinct**.

Scientists are studying Ethiopian wolves to better protect them. This scientist will put a radio collar on this captured Ethiopian wolf, so that he and other scientists can track the wolf after it is released back into the wild.

Plans to Save the Wolves

Scientists have a plan to help the Ethiopian wolves **survive**. First, they want to save more habitat for the wolves. If more of the highland grasslands are protected, the wolves will have more land to live on and more prey to eat. Next, the scientists hope to reduce other **threats**, like those from domestic dogs. They will do this by patrolling the parks and telling people that live near the parks how to care for their dogs. They also want to capture some Ethiopian wolves and bring them into **captivity**. Wolves born in captivity can be returned to areas where wolves have disappeared. If scientists are successful with these efforts, the numbers of Ethiopian wolves in the wild might begin to increase again. If that happens, they will no longer be threatened with extinction.

Glossary

adapted (uh-DAP-tid) Changed to fit new conditions.

captivity (kap-TIH-vih-tee) When an animal lives in a zoo or aquarium instead of in the wild.

environment (en-VY-urn-ment) All of the living things and conditions that make up a place.

extinct (ik-STINKT) To no longer exist.

genes (JEENZ) Many tiny parts on the center of a cell. Genes tell your cells how your body will look and act.

groom (GROOM) To clean someone's body and make it neat and tidy.

habitats (HA-bih-tats) Surroundings where an animal or plant naturally lives.

litter (LIH-tur) A group of baby animals born to the same mother at the same time.

mate (MAYT) When a male and female join together to make babies.

muzzles (MUH-zuhlz) The parts of animals' heads that extend forward and contain the nose.

patrol (puh-TROHL) To make sure an area stays safe.

prey (PRAY) An animal that is hunted by another animal for food.

regurgitated (re-GUR-juh-tay-tid) To have vomited, or thrown up, partly eaten food.

rodents (ROH-dints) Animals with gnawing teeth, such as mice, rats, or squirrels.

survive (sur-VYV) To live longer than; to stay alive.

territory (TEHR-uh-tohr-ee) Land or space protected by an animal for its use.

threats (THREHTS) Things that might cause harm.

Index

A
adapted, 9
Africa, 5, 6, 9

C
captivity, 22

D
den, 17
diet, 10
diseases, 21

E
Ethiopia, 21
extinct(ion), 21, 22

F
food, 5, 9, 13, 17

G
genes, 9
gray wolves('), 5, 6, 9, 10, 13, 15, 18

H
hunt, 5, 10, 14, 15

J
jackals, 6, 9

M
mate(d), 17, 18, 21
muzzle(s), 6, 15, 17

P
pack(s), 5, 10, 13, 14, 15, 17, 18
prey, 9, 10, 13, 14, 22
puppies, 17, 18

R
red wolves, 5
rodents, 6, 9, 10, 13

T
territory, 13, 14, 17

Web Sites

To learn more about Ethiopian wolves, check out these Web sites:
http://users.ox.ac.uk/~wcruinfo/1ethwlf.htm
www.wolf.org